WATCH AND
PRAY WITH ME

WATCH AND PRAY WITH ME

KARL RAHNER

TRANSLATED BY WILLIAM V. DYCH, S.J.

A Crossroad Book

The Crossroad Publishing Company

New York

The Crossroad Publishing Company
370 Lexington Avenue, New York, NY 10017

First English edition,
Herder and Herder, New York, 1966

Original edition,
Heilige Stunde und Passionsandacht,
published by Herder, Freiburg im Breisgau.

IMPRIMI POTEST:
Godfrey Heinzel, S.J.
Praep. Prov. Austriae

NIHIL OBSTAT:
William J. Collins, S.T.L.
Censor Librorum

✠ Ernest J. Primeau
Bishop of Manchester
September 15, 1965

© 1966 by Herder and Herder, Incorporated

Library of Congress Catalog Card Number: 66-13068

ISBN 0-8245-1840-3

Printed in the United States of America

1 2 3 4 5 6 7 8 9 10   04 03 02 01 00

CONTENTS

A HOLY HOUR

THE SEVEN LAST WORDS

A
HOLY
HOUR

1

The Presence of Jesus and His Life

Lord Jesus Christ, Son of the living God, true God and true man, one person in two distinct but undivided natures, we adore You because You are truly present here with us.

You are present here first of all because You are God from all eternity, of one being, one power, and one majesty with the eternal Father, present in all things and all places because of Your infinity, in which all things live and move and have their being.

And You are also present here as man. You are here with us in the Sacrament of the Altar with Your body and soul and with Your human heart. You are present in the Sacrament, You Who were born of the Virgin Mary, lived a human life, and accepted whatever that life brought: the big things and the little things, the joys and the tears, the long, monotonous routine and the moments of greatness. You are present in the Sacrament, You Who suffered under Pontius Pilate and were crucified. You are present in the Sacrament, You Who drank the chalice of suffering to the very dregs on the cross. You are present in that body which was brought back to life and glorified with God's own majesty. You are with us in Your human heart which now experiences the joy of all eternity, and in Your human spirit which now gazes upon the inaccessible light of the Father and His Son and His Holy Spirit, and sees the eternal, Trinitarian God face to face.

You are truly present here as man. When we look, we do not see anything, but the eye of faith sees You, and sees You as our brother, present here with us. When we listen, we do not hear anything, but the ear of faith catches the sound of the eternal hymn of praise which You as High Priest sing to the eternal Father in behalf of all men, a hymn that You will sing forever from a heart now joyful and filled with the glory of God.

We adore You, we praise You, we thank You, we give glory to Your majesty because You wanted to dwell among us, You Who are our God, Who are our origin and our beginning, our end and our destination. We thank You because You wanted to dwell among us as a man just like ourselves. We thank You because You wanted to be born as we are born, to make Your way as a pilgrim through the narrow confines of our creatureliness and through the valley of our tears, and to reach Your end and destination by going through all this as we must do, You Who are the end and destination of all things.

You are present with us. And hence Your human life is present with us, closer to us than we can imagine. Seen in their deepest reality, all the things that made up Your life nineteen hundred years ago are only apparently past. To be sure, the earthly surface of Your life is past. You will never again be born as a poor child; now You never get hungry and thirsty, You never get tired, You never cry. The multicolored, ever-changing nothingness that we call human life does not pass by You any more as it once did, no longer courses through Your soul to change You and to leave its mark on You. You do not die any more. All that is over and past for You, and its value lies precisely in its being unique and transitory. All these things are past now, for even that part of You which is human, created, finite, and mutable has passed over into the eternity of the Father, has reached the goal that is its fulfillment, where all change reaches its fulfillment in what is final and definitive. It is there that reality is freest and

11

most alive, where the whole course of time is drawn up into the single "now" of eternity which encompasses everything in a single instant. Your temporal, human life is past, but in becoming past it has passed over into God.

And for this reason it remains present in its deepest reality. For Your human life is now perfectly united with the eternal God Who is the origin of all things and in Whose wisdom and love everything past is eternally and unalterably present. Your human spirit and Your human heart see and embrace Him in Whom all time has its eternity, all becoming its everlasting permanence, all change its endless stability, and the whole past its eternal present. In the eternal wisdom and love of God Himself Your heart continually sees and loves, acknowledges and embraces the presence of Your past life in God, for in God that life has its fullest presence.

But also in Your heart itself, O Jesus, Your past life is still present in a very real sense.

For what passes in a human life is merely the external event. But when this event sinks into the darkness of past nothingness, it gives birth to something eternal. It contributes its part to the formation of the spiritual man in us, and that man is eternal. In the passage of time there comes to be in us something that does not pass away. We are not like a street, on which the endless stream of moments passes and then is just as empty as it ever was, once the moments have passed. We are much more like a storehouse, in which every moment leaves something behind as it passes, namely that part of it which is eternal: the uniqueness of a free act of love, the finality of a man's decision for or against God. For these are timeless realities. It is as though the waves of time break silently against the shores of eternity in their constant ebb and flow, and as though every wave, every moment, every deed leaves behind that part of itself which is eternal: its goodness or its evil. For these are the eternal elements in the things of time.

This eternal goodness or evil of our past actions sinks down into the eternal ground of our soul, penetrates into it, and gives shape to the hidden core of our soul. It is hidden from us, of course, not from God. And so there is gradually formed in the passage of time something eternal, the countenance of our soul that is to last forever, and in that countenance our eternal destiny is decided. When time reaches the end of its course, everything is not really over and done with. For then the waters of transitoriness are merely drained off, leaving behind and revealing to the eyes of man what had been hidden: his life as he has freely formed and fashioned it for its eternal existence.

So it is also with You, O Jesus, for You are truly a man. You really lived a human life. And so this whole life remains present in You as well as in God. You are at this moment and forever the person that You came to be throughout the course of Your life. Your childhood is past, but You are still at this moment a person Who has lived through a childhood. You are now what only someone Who was once a child can be. Your tears are dried up, but You are now what only someone can be Who has once cried, Whose heart can never forget the reasons for its tears. Your sufferings are past, but the maturity of a man Who has suffered is Yours forever. Your earthly life and death are past, but what came to be through them exists for all eternity, and so is present with us. The courage of Your life which overcame all things has an eternal presence, and so does the love which animated and transfigured Your life. Your heart and its response of total surrender to the incomprehensible will of the Father has an eternal presence, and also Your obedience, Your fidelity, Your meekness, and Your love for sinners. All of these grew and became strong through all the moments of Your life, and, because You freely embraced them, they have entered into the structure of Your real and permanent human self. It is as this person that You are now with us, and so everything that You were and lived and suffered are also present with us.

There is still a third reason why the life that You once lived is present here with us in a very real sense. When You lived Your life on earth, You did not know and love only Your own earthly surroundings, Your own country, and the people who were Your contemporaries. You also knew and loved all of us, and this not only as God, but also in Your human heart. You knew and loved even me, my life, my times, my surroundings, my destiny, my moments of greatness and littleness, all that I have freely chosen to be. You already had a knowledge of all of this in the mysterious interiority at the center of Your being. You had already taken all of this into Your heart and borne it there. And so my life had a share in the formation of Your life. My life belongs to Your destiny. During Your life You had already acknowledged my life, You prayed for me, You cried for me, You gave thanks for the graces I was to receive. Because during Your life You were deeply concerned about me, Your attitude toward me and my life forms part of the reality of Your life. And when Your life entered into eternity and then became present with us in this Sacrament, it gave You a presence with us precisely as the person Whose life, now in its final state, had always included knowledge of me and love for me.

It is as this person that we wish to adore You. O Jesus, we adore You. O eternal God, we adore You.

Our Redeemer, present here in this Sacrament, we adore You.

Jesus, present as true man, we adore You.

Life and death of Jesus, present from all eternity in

the immutable knowledge and will of the eternal Father, we adore You.

Life and death of Jesus, present for all eternity in Your heart which became what it is now, and will be forever in heaven, through this life and death, we adore You.

Life and suffering of Jesus, truly present with us whose lives You already knew and loved during Your life and suffering, we adore You.

Jesus, Who are truly present with us, we adore You.

2

The Presence of Jesus' Agony
in the Garden

Jesus, You are truly here with us. You are with us as man, in flesh and blood, in heart and spirit. And so Your human life is also present here with us, for it is not simply past, but has entered into the eternal reality of Your heart.

And so the hours of Your struggle and suffering in the Garden of Olives are also present with us, and it is these hours that we want to honor in faith and love, in sincerity and gratitude, with compassion and reparation during this hour.

In the glory of heaven Your human spirit sees even

at this moment the Father's eternal, immutable will which appointed for You to live the hours in the Garden of Olives. Your heart is still adoring this will of the Father even now. And Your spirit and Your heart are present with us.

You are with us, You Who endured the agony in the Garden. What You lived through and suffered then is now past: no longer do sadness and anguish, the bitterness and the agony of death touch Your heart, now that it has entered upon the blessedness of the Father. But Your heart is the heart that it is because of what it experienced and suffered then, and all this experience and suffering remain in it. It is with this heart that You are present with us. The Apostle says of You in Hebrews 5:7 that in the days of Your earthly life, with a loud cry and tears, You offered up prayers and supplications to Him Who was able to save You from death, and that You learned obedience from the things that You suffered. It is as this person that we now adore You, and we say to You Who became what You are through Your agony in the garden: have mercy on us.

O Jesus, in the obedience that You learned in the Garden of Olives, have mercy on us.

Jesus, in the resignation that You won by Your struggle in the Garden, have mercy on us.

Jesus, in Your readiness to suffer that was tried and proven in the Garden of Olives, have mercy on us.

18

Jesus, in Your love for us that was not overcome in the Garden of Olives, have mercy on us.

Jesus, in Your goodness that was not embittered even in the Garden of Olives, have mercy on us.

Jesus, in Your courage that remained steadfast even in the Garden of Olives, have mercy on us.

Jesus, in Your meekness that did not falter even in the Garden of Olives, have mercy on us.

Jesus, in the anguish and sorrow of those hours, have mercy on us.

Jesus, in Your fear and trembling, have mercy on us.

Jesus, in the prayer that You offered in the Garden of Olives, have mercy on us.

Jesus, Who fell prostrate on the ground, have mercy on us.

Jesus, Who persevered in prayer again and again, have mercy on us.

Jesus, Whose soul was sad even unto death, have mercy on us.

Jesus, Who prayed that the chalice of suffering might be taken away, have mercy on us.

Jesus, Who said: "Not My will, but Thine be done," have mercy on us.

Jesus, Who cried: "Abba, Father," have mercy on us.

Jesus, Who three times said "yes" to the will of the Father, have mercy on us.

Jesus, Who was abandoned by the sleeping apostles, have mercy on us.

Jesus, Who was comforted by an angel, have mercy on us.

Jesus, Who suffered a bloody sweat in Your agony in the Garden of Olives, have mercy on us.

Jesus, Who knew and suffered in advance all future sufferings, have mercy on us.

Jesus, Who knew the sins of the whole world in the Garden of Olives, have mercy on us.

Jesus, Who felt disgust at the sins of all ages, have mercy on us.

Jesus, Who knew my sins in the Garden of Olives, have mercy on us.

Jesus, Whose heart was saddened by my sins in the Garden of Olives, have mercy on us.

Jesus, Who was willing to take all this upon Yourself in the Garden of Olives, have mercy on us.

Jesus, Whose heart was grieved by the fruitlessness of Your suffering, have mercy on us.

Jesus, Who felt abandoned by God during Your agony in the Garden of Olives, have mercy on us.

Jesus, Who was obedient to the incomprehensible will of the Father, have mercy on us.

Jesus, Whose love for God never wavered though He seemed only to be angry, have mercy on us.

Jesus, Who in the Garden of Olives prayed for all who would ever suffer, have mercy on us.

Jesus, Who in the Garden of Olives was the most abandoned of all the abandoned, have mercy on us.

Jesus, Who in the Garden of Olives spoke for all who cry out to God from their anguish, have mercy on us.

Jesus, Who in the Garden of Olives set an example for all who suffer temptation, have mercy on us.

Jesus, Who in the Garden of Olives gave comfort to all who struggle painfully in the agony of death, have mercy on us.

Jesus, Who in the Garden of Olives was the head of all who must suffer for the sins of the world, have mercy on us.

Jesus, Who in the Garden of Olives shared as a brother in the distress and despair of the whole world, have mercy on us.

Jesus, Who in the Garden of Olives understood all suffering, have mercy on us.

Jesus, Who in the Garden of Olives offered a haven to all who are forsaken, have mercy on us.

Jesus, Who in the Garden of Olives still loved every sinner, have mercy on us.

Jesus, Who in the Garden of Olives still wanted to press to Your heart the most condemned, have mercy on us.

Jesus, Whose agony in the Garden of Olives redeemed our death and made it a happy homecoming, have mercy on us.

Jesus in the Garden of Olives, be merciful to us: spare us, O Jesus.

Jesus in the Garden of Olives, be merciful to us: deliver us, O Jesus.

From the sins that You wept for in the Garden of Olives, deliver us, O Jesus.

From ingratitude for Your love, deliver us, O Jesus.

From indifference to Your suffering, deliver us, O Jesus.

From a lack of compassion for Your agony and death, deliver us, O Jesus.

From resistance to the grace that You won for us in the Garden of Olives, deliver us, O Jesus.

From rejecting Your acceptance of suffering and expiation in the Garden of Olives, deliver us, O Jesus.

From doubt about God's love during our own nights in the Garden of Olives, deliver us, O Jesus.

From bitterness over our own bitter agony in the Garden of Olives, deliver us, O Jesus.

From despair in our moments of abandonment, deliver us, O Jesus.

We poor sinners, we pray You, hear us.

Forgive us our sins, we pray You, hear us.

Give us an understanding of Your suffering, we pray You, hear us.

Teach us Your surrender to the will of the Father in the Garden of Olives, we pray You, hear us.

Give us Your perseverance in prayer during the

night of Your agony in the Garden, we pray You, hear us.

Give us the dispositions of Your heart during those hours in the Garden of Olives, we pray You, hear us.

Grant us an understanding of penance and reparation, we pray You, hear us.

Let us recognize our suffering as a share in Your holy suffering, we pray You, hear us.

Fill us with Your disgust for our sins, we pray You, hear us.

Give us Your strength and patience in our trials and abandonment, we pray You, hear us.

Let Your courage in the face of death be with us in our own death-agony, we pray You, hear us.

Send us Your consoling angel at the hour of our death, we pray You, hear us.

Teach us to watch and to pray with You always in the Garden of Olives, we pray You, hear us.

Teach us to pray when we feel weak and discouraged, we pray You, hear us.

Put into our hearts and upon our lips the name "Father," especially when God seems to be only the Lord, the stern judge, and the incomprehensible, unapproachable God, we pray You, hear us.

Lamb of God, Who takes away the sins of the world, spare us, O Lord.

Lamb of God, Who takes away the sins of the world, hear us, O Lord.

Lamb of God, Who takes away the sins of the world, have mercy on us.

Let us pray: Jesus, Who are present here, as we consider the holy dispositions of Your divine and human heart, those dispositions in which You suffered the agony in the Garden of Olives in reparation, obedience, and love, and with which You dwell among us even now, we say this prayer to You: fill our hearts with sorrow for our sins; let us in union with You take up our crosses in a spirit of penance and reparation; and grant that we may gratefully return the love that You have shown us, that love which prompted You to endure Your most holy sufferings in the Garden of Olives for us sinners. Amen.

3

The Presence of the Agony
in the Garden in Us

Lord Jesus Christ, You are present here in this holy Sacrament. But this is not the only way that You dwell among us. You also live within us. Ever since we were incorporated by baptism into Your Mystical Body, which is the Church, You live within us by Your Holy Spirit. He has anointed us and sealed us. And so You are the life of our life, the life of our spirit, the life of our heart. In the strength and life-giving power of Your Holy Spirit, Who proceeds from the Father through You, You have taken hold of the most hidden depths of our soul, the innermost center of our being. You have transformed and glorified it; You have made it holy and divine.

It is no longer we who live, but You Who lives in us. We no longer belong to ourselves. We belong to You. You are the law of our life, the interior strength of our being and our actions, the hidden light of our spirit, the flame that burns in the depths of our heart, the holy splendor of our whole being. We have been transfigured by the eternal light of God Himself.

You exist and live in us; You share Your own being and life with us through Your presence as uncreated Grace; You give us the power through created grace to receive You and the one, Trinitarian God, and thus to live Your life, the life of God. For these reasons we are really and truly sons and daughters of Your eternal Father. By the grace of Your incomprehensible love, we are really Your brothers and sisters, co-heirs with You of the glory of Your Father, that glory which the Father communicates to You as God in His eternal act of generation. He also bestows that glory on Your human soul by grace, just as He bestows it on us. And so we are really filled with that eternal love which proceeds from You and from the Father as the person of the Holy Spirit.

You live in us so very much, O Jesus, that even Your presence in the Sacrament is only the means by which you declare, communicate, increase, and strengthen Your presence in us by grace. Your presence in the Sacrament will last only until the end of time, but Your presence within us will remain forever. As soon as the veil of faith that hides it falls away, Your presence will rise up from those depths of our heart which are hidden from us now, and will then become our eternal life.

But since You live within us, our life is subject to the law of Your life, even down to what are seemingly the smallest details of our life in the world. Our life is a continuation of Your life. When we were baptized, a new chapter in Your life began; our baptismal certificate is a page from the history of Your life. So we must fashion ourselves after Your image, You Who are the first-born of many brothers. We must even "put You on." Since You live within us, Your image must become more and more manifest in us. God's hidden grace in Your human soul made Your earthly life a pure expression and revelation of itself in the world of earthly phenomena. So too must this same grace—Your grace—make our lives, all that we do and suffer, a revelation of grace, and thus make our earthly life conformed to Your earthly and heavenly life. You wanted to live Your life in every age, in every situation, among all peoples and generations. Since You could not do this within the narrow, created confines of Your own earthly life, You take hold of our lives by Your grace and by Your Holy Spirit. He comes to us through Your pierced heart to try to make our lives like Yours.

27

In this way, O Jesus, Your life lives on in ever new forms and expressions always and everywhere until the end of time.

But if Your life is to express itself anew in our lives by Your grace and by Your Holy Spirit, then this is true even of Your suffering, of Your blessed passion. For this is the decisive event in Your life. In baptism we were baptized into Your death, as the Apostle says. Since we are the children of God, filled with Your Spirit, and co-heirs with You, we must suffer with You and thus win a share in Your glory. The Apostle says that we bear always Your suffering in our body, so that Your life might become manifest in our mortal flesh. Since You are the crucified, it is as the crucified that You must manifest Yourself in us. You continue to suffer in the members of Your Mystical Body until the end of time. Not until the last tear has been shed, the last pain suffered, and the last death-agony endured will Your suffering, O Jesus, really be finished. If Your cross does not weigh also upon me, I cannot be Your disciple. If Your suffering does not become my portion also, I must admit that the spirit and the law of Your earthly life are not dwelling and working in me. And then I would not belong to You. I would be far from You, Who are my true and eternal life.

You want to continue Your sufferings in me for my own salvation and that of the whole world, and for the glory of Your Father. By my sufferings and agony,

You want to fill up what is wanting in Your sufferings for Your Body, which is the Church. And so I shall receive in my life again and again a share in Your agony in the Garden of Olives, a very small share, but nevertheless a real one. My "holy hours," those hours when I honor Your agony in the Garden of Olives, will be made in the truest sense not during the peaceful hours of these pious devotions here in church. My real "holy hours" are those hours when sufferings of body and soul come to overwhelm me. Those hours when God hands me the chalice of suffering. Those hours when I weep for my sins. Those hours when I call out to Your Father, O Jesus, and do not seem to be heard. Those hours when faith becomes agonizingly difficult, hope seems to be giving way to despair, and love seems to have died in my heart. They are the real "holy hours" in my life, those hours when Your grace working in my heart draws me mysteriously into Your agony in the garden. When those hours come upon me, O Lord, have mercy on me.

When Your agony in the Garden of Olives over-shadows my life, stand at my side. Give me then the grace to realize that those holy hours of Yours are a grace, that they are hours of Your life, of Your agony in the Garden of Olives. And let me understand at that moment that in the final analysis they come upon me not through blind chance, not through the wickedness of men, not through tragic fate. They come rather as the grace to share in Your destiny, which was to suffer in the Garden of Olives.

Give me then the grace to say "yes," "yes" to even the most bitter hours, "yes" to everything, for everything that happens in those hours, even what results from my own guilt, is the will of Him Who is eternal love. May He be blest forever. Give me in those hours the grace to pray, even if the heavens appear leaden and closed, even if the deathly silence of God falls upon me like a tomb, even if all the stars of my life flicker out, even if faith and love seem to have died in my heart, even if my lips stammer out words of prayer which ring as lies in my lifeless heart. In those hours Your grace is still within me, and may it transform the chilling despair that seeks to destroy my heart into an act of faith in the reality of Your love. In those hours may the annihilating weakness of a soul in its death-agony, a soul with nothing left to cling to, become a cry to Your Father in heaven. In those moments—let me say it while I kneel before You—let everything merge into and be embraced by Your agony unto death in the Garden of Olives.

Have mercy on us, O Jesus, when the angel of our lives hands us the chalice as he handed it to You. Have mercy on us at that moment, but not by taking the chalice away from us. Anyone who belongs to You must drink it with You as You drank it. Rather, have mercy on us by being with us, not to make us feel

30

strong during those hours, but that Your strength might be victorious in our weakness. Have mercy on us, we pray you. During Your agony in the Garden of Olives you saw before You all who would ever suffer through such hours in the Garden, and this sight gave comfort to Your heart. Grant that we might belong to the number of those who were Your consolation in that hour. This is the mercy that we ask of You.

When You share with us the hours of Your agony in the Garden of Olives, have mercy on us.

When we should recognize the hours of our suffering as a sharing in Your agony, have mercy on us.

When God's will seems difficult and incomprehensible to us, have mercy on us.

When sorrow and sadness, disgust and anguish overshadow us as they did You, have mercy on us.

When sorrow for our sins comes upon us, have mercy on us.

When the holiness and justice of God fills us with terror, have mercy on us.

When we must do penance and make reparation for our failures, have mercy on us.

When we are called upon to share in the sufferings of Your Mystical Body, the Church, have mercy on us.

When we are tempted out of selfishness to exaggerate our suffering and to pity ourselves, have mercy on us.

When we are betrayed by friends as You were, have mercy on us.

When we are left without help as You were, have mercy on us.

When we meet hatred with hostility as You did, have mercy on us.

When our love receives only ingratitude in return, have mercy on us.

When the Father does not seem to hear our prayer, have mercy on us.

When the light of faith seems to be going out during our night of suffering, have mercy on us.

When hope seems to be giving way to despair during our hours in the Garden of Olives, have mercy on us.

When God's love seems to have died in us during our real "holy hours," have mercy on us.

When nothing else lives on in us except our final misery, our complete powerlessness, and the incomprehensibility of God, have mercy on us.

When the agony of death strikes us as it did You, have mercy on us.

Lamb of God, Who took upon Yourself all our suffering in the Garden of Olives, spare us, O Jesus.

Lamb of God, Who redeemed and sanctified our suffering in the Garden of Olives and on the cross, hear us, O Jesus.

Lamb of God, Who accompanies into the glory of the Father all who suffer with You and in You, have mercy on us, O Jesus. Amen.

THE
SEVEN
LAST
WORDS

Preparatory Prayer

Lord Jesus Christ, our Savior and Redeemer, I kneel before Your blessed cross. I want to open my spirit and my heart to contemplate Your holy sufferings. I want to place Your cross before my poor soul that I might know it a little better, that I might receive more deeply into my heart all that You did and suffered, and that I might realize who it was for whom You suffered. May Your grace be with me, the grace to shake off the coldness and indifference of my heart, to forget my everyday life for at least this half-hour, and to dwell with You in love, sorrow, and gratitude. King of all hearts, may Your crucified love embrace my poor, weak, tired, and discouraged heart. Fill my heart with an interior awareness of You. Stir up in me what I need so badly: compassion for You, love for You, honesty and fidelity, and perseverance in the contemplation of Your holy sufferings and death.

I want to meditate upon Your seven last words upon the cross, the last words You spoke before You entered into the silence of earthly death, You Who are the Word of God from eternity to eternity. You spoke them with parched lips and out of an anguished heart, those words which came straight from Your heart at the very end. You spoke them to everyone. You spoke them even to me. Let them penetrate into my heart. Right to its very core. Right to its very center. That I might understand them. That I might never again forget them. That they might live in me and become the strength of my lifeless heart. Speak them Yourself to me, so deeply that I feel Your voice vibrating within me.

You will be speaking to me someday at the moment of my death, and even after my death. Those words will be either an eternal beginning, or an everlasting end for me. O Lord, let me hear words of mercy and love from You at the moment of my death. I shall not ignore those words. Let me, therefore, here and now open my heart to receive Your last words upon the cross.

Father, Forgive Them,
for They Know Not What They Do

LUKE 23:34

You are hanging upon the cross. You nailed Your-self to it. You are not going to come down any more from this pole suspending You between heaven and earth. Your body aches from its many wounds. The crown of thorns is tormenting Your head. Blood is running down into Your eyes. The wounds in Your hands and feet burn as though Your limbs were pierced with a white-hot iron. And Your soul is a sea of sorrow, anguish, and hopelessness.

Those who prepared all this for You stand there beneath the cross. They will not even go away and let

You die alone. They stand around. They laugh. They decide that they were right, that the very condition You are in is the clearest proof that what they did to You has satisfied divine justice. They have rendered to God a service of which they should be proud. And so they laugh. They mock. They blaspheme.

A feeling of despair at the sight of such wickedness comes over You, a feeling more terrible than all the pain in Your body. Are there men capable of such wickedness? Do You have anything in common with such men as this? Can one man torture another to death like this? Torture him to death with lies, wickedness, treachery, hypocrisy, and malice, and yet keep up the appearance of righteousness, the air of innocence, the pose of impartial judges? Does God let this happen in His world? Can Satan, laughing and sneering, force his way into God's world so jauntily and so sure of victory? O Lord, in such a situation our hearts would have been crushed under the weight of terrible despair. We would have fled from the devil, and from God too. We would have cried out, and frantically pulled at the nails with our hands so that we could once again clench our fists in anger.

But You said: "Father, forgive them, for they know not what they do." You are really a mystery, O Jesus. Where in all Your tortured and tormented soul did You find a place for words like these? Yes, You are a mystery. You love Your enemies. You recommend them to Your Father. You pray for them. And my Lord, if it is not blasphemous to say it, You pardon them with the most implausible excuse there is: they did not know what they were doing. Really they knew it all. But they did not want to know it! And what a person does not want to know he does know in spite of himself, in the deepest, most hidden recesses of his heart. But he hates this knowledge and so refuses to let it come into the clear light of consciousness. And You say: "They did not know what they were doing." But there is one thing that they really did not know: Your love for them. Only the man who loves You can know Your love for him. For it is only upon the man who gives love that there dawns an understanding of the love he has received.

Speak these merciful words of Your boundless love over my sins also. Say to the Father in my behalf: "Forgive him, for he did not know what he was doing." Really I did know it. I knew all of it. But Your love I did not know.

Let me also recall Your first word on the cross when I thoughtlessly mention in the Our Father that I forgive those who have committed wrongs against me. O my God hanging on the cross, if anyone really has wronged me, I am not sure that I could forgive him. And so I need Your strength to pardon and forgive with all my heart those whom in my pride and selfishness I consider my enemies.

41

Amen I Say to You, This Day You Will Be with Me in Paradise

LUKE 23:43

You are now in the agony of death, Your heart is filled to the brim with anguish, and yet You still have a place in that heart for the sufferings of another. You are at the point of death, and yet You are concerned about a criminal, who even in his agony must admit that the hellish pangs of his death are but the just punishment for his evil life. You see Your Mother standing there, but You speak first to the prodigal son. A feeling that God has abandoned You is oppressing You, but You speak of paradise. Your eyes are growing dark in the night of death, but they still see the light of eternity. In death, man's only concern is with himself, for then he is all alone, all by himself. But Your concern is with the souls that are going to enter Your kingdom with You. How merciful is Your heart! How strong and courageous it is!

A miserable criminal asks You to remember him. And You promise him paradise. Is everything going to be different after You die? Will a life of sin and vice be transformed this quickly when You draw near it? When You speak the words of transformation over a life, will even the sins and hateful wickedness of a criminal's life be so transformed by grace that there is nothing left to keep him from approaching the all-holy God?

Surely we too would have admitted some small measure of good will in a robber and criminal like him. But evil habits and vicious instincts, brutality, filth, and meanness, all these do not vanish because of a little good will and a passing feeling of regret in someone on the gallows. Such a man does not enter heaven as quickly as penitents and people who have purified themselves for a long time, people like the saints who have only to sanctify their bodies and souls and make them worthy of the thrice-holy God. But You utter the all-powerful word of Your grace and it goes straight to the heart of this robber. It transforms the hell-fire of his death-agony into the purifying flame of divine love. This divine love transfigures in an instant all that remains of the work of the Father, and consumes all the evil and guilt that keeps God from entering his heart.

Will You also give me the grace never to lose the courage to be bold enough to ask and expect anything from Your goodness? The courage to say, even if I were the most condemned criminal: "Lord, remember me when You come into Your kingdom." O Lord, let Your cross be set up at my death-bed. And let Your lips say to me also: "Amen I say to you, this day you will be with Me in paradise." This word itself would make me worthy to enter the kingdom of Your Father, render me completely forgiven and sanctified by the purifying power of a death in You and with You.

Woman, Behold Your Son;
Son, Behold Your Mother
John 19:26

Now, at the hour of death, the moment has come when Your Mother should again be with You. Now is not the time for her to ask You for a miracle, but it is the time for You to die, and so she should be there. For she was the one to whom You said: "Woman, what do you want Me to do? My hour is not yet come." Now the hour is come, and the Son and the Mother will share it. This is the hour of farewell, the hour of dying. This is the hour when the Mother, who is a widow, is to lose her only Son.

And so once again Your eyes glance down to Your

Mother. You have spared this Mother nothing. You were not only the joy of her life, but also the bitterness and suffering of her life. But both of these were Your grace, for both were Your love. And because in both she stayed at Your side and served You, You love her. Not until she did this was she really Your Mother in the fullest sense. For Your brothers and sisters and Mother are they who do the will of Your Father Who is in heaven.

Even here in Your agony Your love is quick to express the tenderness which in this world every son feels for his mother. And through Your death even the tender, precious things of our world such as this are consecrated and sanctified, these things which make the heart gentle and the earth beautiful. They do not die in Your heart even when it is being crushed in death. And so they are redeemed for heaven. There will be a new earth because even in death You loved the earth, because even while dying for our eternal salvation You were touched by the tears Your Mother was shedding, because even while giving up Your life so that the earth could be made whole You were anxious about a widow, and gave a son to a mother and a mother to a son.

But she does not stand there beneath Your cross merely with the lonely sorrow of a mother whose son is being put to death. She stands there also in our name. She stands there as the Mother of all the living. She gives up her Son in our behalf. It was in our name that she spoke her *"fiat"* to the death of the Lord. She was the Church under the cross; she was the race of the children of Eve; she was fighting the whole world's struggle between the serpent and the Son of the woman. And so, if You gave this Mother to the disciple whom You loved, You gave her to all of us.

You are saying also to me: "Son, daughter, behold your Mother." O word that gave us a legacy that will last forever! Only the man who takes Your Mother as his own from that hour can stand under Your cross, O Jesus, as the disciple whom You love. And all the grace merited by Your death comes to us through the pure hands of this Mother. Say to her as You look upon my poor soul: "Woman, behold your son; Mother, behold your daughter."

Only a pure, virgin heart like the heart of this Mother could have given its consent in the name of the whole world to the marriage of the Lamb with its bride, the Church, the whole human race purchased and purified by Your blood. If I let myself be entrusted by You to the heart of Your Mother, Your death will not be lost on me. And then I shall be present to see the day of Your eternal nuptials dawn, that day when all creation will be made new and united with You forever.

My God, My God, Why Have You Forsaken Me?

MATTHEW 27:46

Death is drawing ever closer. I do not say the end of life on this earth, for that is salvation and peace. But death, and death is the ultimate depths, the unimaginable depths of destruction and agony. Death is drawing near, and death is emptiness, terrible weakness, crushing solitude. In death everything disintegrates, everything slips away, and only forsakenness remains, a forsakenness full of pain and yet unspeakably numbing.

In this night of the senses and of the spirit, in this desert that consumes everything in Your heart, Your soul is still in prayer. The dreadful wasteland of a heart devastated by suffering becomes in You a solitary call to God. O prayer of anguish, prayer of abandonment, prayer of unfathomable weakness, prayer of a forsaken God, let us adore You. If You prayed like this, O Jesus, if You prayed in such an agony, is there any abyss so deep that we cannot call out from it to Your Father? Is there any despair so hopeless that it cannot become a prayer by being encompassed within Your abandonment? Is there any anguish so numbing that it must no longer expect its mute cries to be heard amidst heaven's jubilation?

To express Your anguish, to utter the prayer of Your total abandonment, You began to say the twenty-first psalm. For Your words: "God, My God, why have You forsaken Me?" are the first verse of this ancient lamentation which Your Holy Spirit Himself once put into the heart and upon the lips of a holy man of the Old Testament to express his anguish. And so, if I dare speak this way, the only prayer that You wanted to say during this most bitter agony was one that had been prayed thousands and thousands of years ago. In a sense You prayed in the words of the liturgy when You offered Your own solemn Mass, that Mass in which You offered Yourself as an eternal sacrifice. And in those words You were able to say everything that had to be said. Teach me to pray in the words of Your Church in such a way that they become the words of my own heart.

I Thirst

John the Evangelist, who heard this word himself, says this about it: "Knowing that everything was now accomplished, that the Scripture might be fulfilled, You said: 'I thirst'." Here too You have made Your own a verse from the Psalms which the Spirit of God uttered in prophecy about Your future sufferings. For the same twenty-first Psalm says of You: "My throat is dry as a potsherd and My tongue sticks to My jaws." And in Psalm 69:22 it says of You: "In My thirst they gave Me vinegar to drink."

O Servant of the Father, obedient unto death, even

the death of the cross, You look at everything that is happening to You, and then at what is supposed to be happening to You; at everything You are doing, and then at what You should be doing; at all the actual events and then at what should be. Even here in the agony of death, which usually darkens the spirit and prevents any clear reflection, You are in a sense anxiously concerned that everything in Your life be in harmony with the eternal image that exists in the mind of the Father when He thinks of You.

And so in saying these words Your real concern is not the nameless thirst of Your body that is now bleeding to death and covered with burning wounds, naked and exposed to the scorching, Oriental sun at mid-day. You are telling us, rather, that even here in death, with an almost incomprehensible humility that demands our worship, You are faithful to the will of the Father: "Yes, even what the lips of the prophet foretold of Me as the will of the Father is fulfilled. Yes, truly I thirst." O noble heart, for You even the senseless fury of the pain tormenting Your body is but the fulfillment of Your mission from above.

But You have approached all Your suffering with all its terrible severity with this same attitude. It was a mission, not blind fate. It was the will of the Father, not the wickedness of men. It was the saving act of Your love, not the deed of sinners. You were lost that we might be saved; You died that we might live; You thirsted that we might find refreshment in the waters of life. You were tormented by thirst that from the heart in Your pierced side there might flow streams of living water. You invited all to come to this heart when You cried out with a loud voice on the feast of tabernacles: "If anyone thirst, let him who believes in Me come to Me and drink. For from the heart of the Messiah shall flow streams of the living waters of the spirit."

You thirsted for me, You thirsted after my love and my salvation: as the deer thirsts for the spring, so does my soul thirst for you.

It Is Finished

JOHN 19:30

You really said: "It is fulfilled." Yes, Lord, Your end has come. The end of Your life. The end of Your honor, the end of Your human hope, the end of Your struggle and labor. Everything is over and done. Everything has been emptied out. Your life has run its course. You are hopeless and powerless. But this end is Your fulfillment. For whoever comes to the end in love and fidelity has reached fulfillment. Your failure is Your triumph.

O Lord, when shall I once and for all grasp this, this law of Your life and so of my life? The law that death is life, losing oneself is finding oneself, poverty is riches, and suffering is a grace, that to reach the end in truth is fulfillment.

Yes, You have reached fulfillment. The mission that Your Father gave You is fulfilled. The chalice that was not to pass from You has been drunk. The death that was so terrible has been endured. The redemption of the world is accomplished. Death is conquered. Sin is vanquished. The power of the spirit of darkness is broken. The gateway to life is open. The freedom of the sons of God is won. The quickening Spirit of grace can now breathe where He will. Already the horizon of this dark world is slowly beginning to grow red as the dawn of Your love breaks upon it. And in only a little while—the little while that we call the history of the world—it will burst into flame, the clear flame of the fire of Your Godhead. And then the whole world will be plunged into the flaming sea of Your love. All is finished.

Bring me to fulfillment in Your Spirit, You Who brought the whole world to completion, Who are the Word of the Father Who brought all things to fulfillment by becoming flesh and accepting its torments.

Shall I too be able to say someday in the twilight of my life: "It is finished; I have accomplished the mission You gave me to do"? When the shadows of death fall upon me, shall I be able to pray after You the words of Your high-priestly prayer: "Father, the hour is come

. . . I have glorified You on earth by accomplishing the work You gave Me to do. And now, Father, do Thou glorify Me with Thyself"? O Jesus, may the mission the Father has given me be whatever He wants it to be—great or small, sweet or bitter, life or death. Grant that I might accomplish it as You did. For You have already brought everything to completion, including my life, so that I can complete it.

Father, into Your Hands
I Commend My Spirit

LUKE 23:46

O Jesus, utterly forsaken, tormented by suffering, You have come to the end. To that end where everything is taken away, even one's soul and his freedom to say "yes" or "no," and hence where man is taken from himself. For that is what death is. Who or what does the taking? Nothing? Blind fate? Merciless nature? No, it is the Father! God, Who is wisdom and love! And so You let Yourself be taken from Yourself. You give Yourself over with confidence into those gentle, invisible hands. We who are weak in faith and fearful for our own selves experience those hands as the sudden, grasping, merciless, stifling grip of blind fate and of death. But You know that they are the hands of the Father. And Your eyes, now grown dark in death, can still see the Father. They look up into the large, peaceful eyes of His love, and from Your lips come the last words of Your life: "Father, into Your hands I commend My spirit."

You give everything to Him Who gave everything to You. You put everything into the hands of Your Father without guarantee and without reservations. That is doing a great deal, and it is a hard and bitter thing to do. All alone You had to bear the burden of Your life: all men, their meanness, Your mission, Your cross, failure and death. But now the time for enduring is past. Now You can put everything and Yourself into the hands of the Father. Everything. Those hands are so gentle and so sure. They are like the hands of a Mother. They embrace Your soul as one would lift a little bird carefully and lovingly into his hands. Now nothing is difficult any more, everything is easy, everything is light and grace. And everything is safe and secure in the heart of God, where one can cry all his anguish out, and the Father will kiss away the tears from the cheeks of His child.

O Jesus, will You one day put my poor soul and my poor life also into the hands of the Father? Put everything there, the burden of my life, and the burden of my sins, not on the scales of justice, but into the hands of the Father. Where should I flee, where should I seek refuge, if not at Your side? For You are my brother in bitter moments, and You suffered for my sins. See, I come to You today. I kneel beneath Your cross. I kiss the feet which follow me down the wandering path of my life constantly and silently, leaving bloody footprints behind.

I embrace Your cross, Lord of eternal love, heart of all hearts, heart that was pierced, heart that is patient and unspeakably kind. Have mercy on me. Receive me into Your love. And when I come to the end of my pilgrimage, when the day begins to decline and the shadows of death surround me, speak Your last word at the end of my life also: "Father, into Your hands I commend his spirit." O good Jesus. Amen.